My Dad / Mom is A.....
Book of Occupations
(Kiddie Learning)

Speedy Publishing LLC
40 E. Main St. #1156
Newark, DE 19711
www.speedypublishing.com

When I grow up, I want to be a

____

because

____

____

My mom is a television reporter.

My mom is an astronaut.

My mom is
a writer.

My dad is a sculptor.

My dad is an architect.

My mom is
a doctor.

My dad is an
IT expert.

My mom is an optometrist.

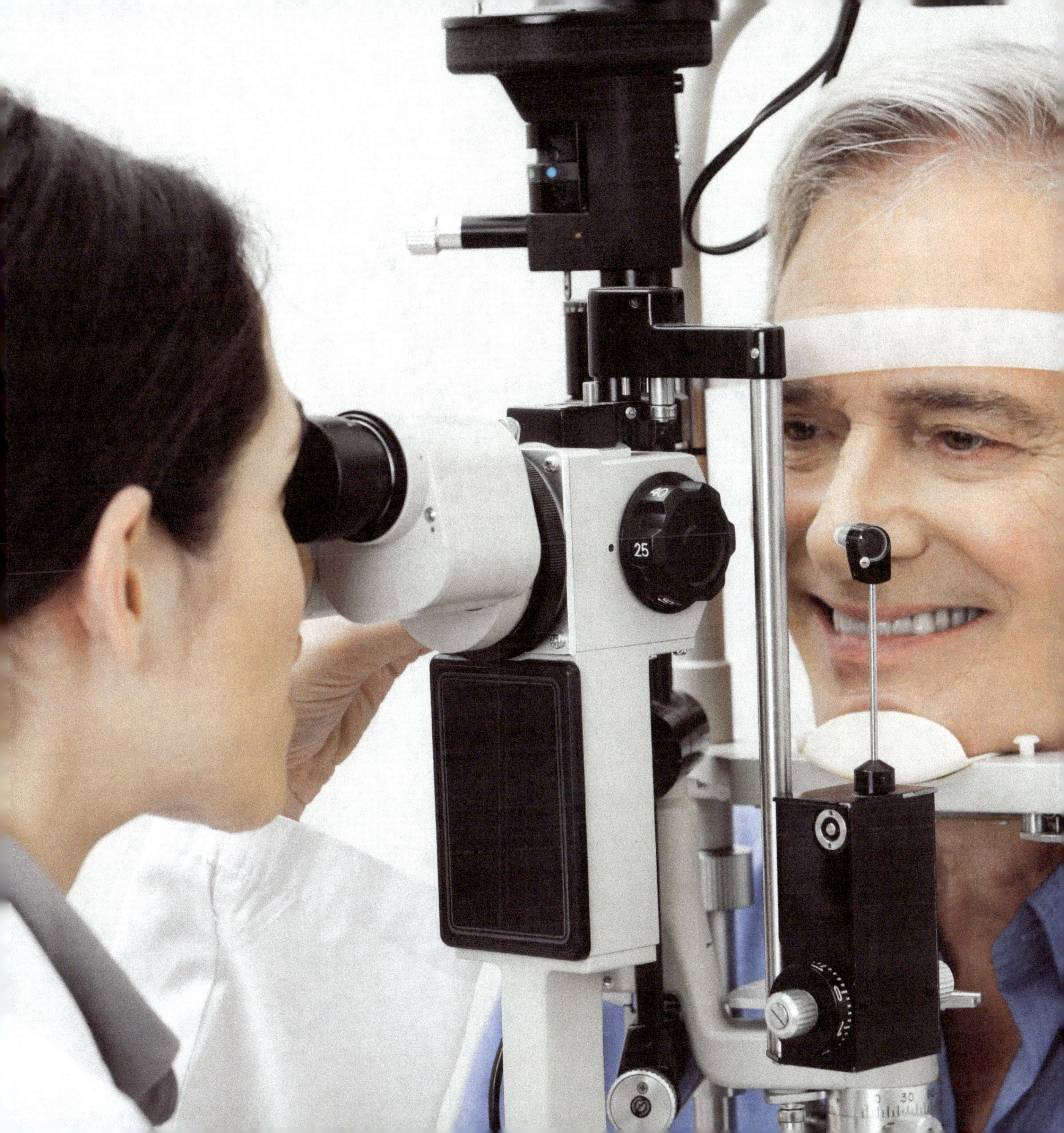
40
25

My mom is a ballroom dancer.

My dad is a biologist.

My dad is a musician.

My dad is a filmmaker.

My mom is a hair dresser.

My mom is a graphic artist.

www.ingramcontent.com/pod-product-compliance
Lightning Source LLC
LaVergne TN
LVHW060833170826
845678LV00010B/1974

* 9 7 9 8 8 6 9 4 5 2 0 5 4 *